Cursive Handwriting Practice Workbook for Boys

Julie Harper

Cursive Handwriting Practice Workbook for Boys

Copyright © 2013 by Julie Harper

Cover Design by Melissa Stevens
www.theillustratedauthor.net
Write. Create. Illustrate.

Children's Books > Education & Reference > Words & Language
Children's Books > Education & Reference > Education > Workbooks

ISBN 10: 1492323101
EAN 13: 978-1492323105

Table of Contents

Introduction

The goal of this workbook is to inspire boys' interest in learning and practicing cursive handwriting. Boys enjoy reading phrases like "monster trucks" and sentences like, "Keep your eye on the ball." Exercises like these help to make learning fun, whether in the classroom or at home.

This Cursive Handwriting Practice Workbook for Boys focuses on writing phrases and sentences in cursive. Students who need more practice writing individual letters or single words may benefit from using this workbook in combination with a basic cursive writing workbook which focuses on practicing letters and short words.

Three sections of this workbook help students develop their cursive writing skills in three parts:
- ✓ Part 1 has mostly short phrases. Students trace and copy the words.
- ✓ Part 2 advances onto sentences. Students trace and copy the words.
- ✓ Part 3 just involves copying; there is no tracing at this stage.

May your students or children improve their handwriting skills and enjoy reading and writing these boy-themed phrases and sentences.

Uppercase Cursive Alphabet

A B C D E F

G H I J K L

M N O P Q R

S T U V W X

Y Z

Lowercase Cursive Alphabet

a   b   c   d   e   f

g   h   i   j   k   l

m   n   o   p   q   r

s   t   u   v   w   x

y   z

Part 1 Short Phrases

Part 1 Instructions: First trace each word and then copy the words onto the blank line below.

Hot rod

Hot rod

Drag race

Drag race

Pace car

Race car

Checkered flag

Checkered flag

Wizardry

Wizardry

Sorcery

Sorcery

Spellbook

Spellbook

Potions

Potions

Magic wand

Magic wand

Spider

Spider

Beetle

Beetle

Stink bug

Stink

Caterpillar

Caterpillar

Tarantula

Tarantula

Castle

Castle

Knight

Knight

Jousting

Jousting

Swords

Swords

Shining armor

Shining armor

Baseball

Baseball

Football

Football

Soccer

Soccer

Basketball

Basketball

Hockey

Hockey

Super hero

Cape and mask

Special powers

Good versus evil

Secret identity

Werewolf

Vampire

Zombie

Ghostly apparition

Headless horseman

Dump truck

Pickup truck

Monster truck

Garbage truck

Sport utility vehicle

Tow truck

Paramedics

Ambulance

Fire engine

Police motorcycle

Jacks

Marbles

Kick the can

Tag, you're it

Hide-and-seek

Jet airplane

Helicopter

Rocket ship

Space shuttle

Hang glider

Hiking

Backpack

Campfire

Wilderness

Pup tent

Cowboy

Indian

Sheriff

Saddle

Canteen

Wrench

Hammer

Toolbox

Screwdriver

Nuts and bolts

Snowman

Snow angels

Sledding

Snowboarding

Snowball fight

Unicycle

Skateboard

Roller skates

Motorcycle

Mountain bike

Home run

Touchdown

Field goal

Slam dunk

Hole-in-one

Zip line

Dirt skiing

Parachuting

Rock climbing

Obstacle course

Crane

Backhoe

Forklift

Bulldozer

Cement mixer

Coach

Referee

Umpire

Trainer

Scorekeeper

Flip

Wheelie

No hands

Bunny hop

Three-sixty

Handstand

Cartwheel

Back flip

Handspring

Somersault

Pitcher

Catcher

Shortstop

Batter

Outfielder

Fireman

Astronaut

Police officer

Medical doctor

Airline pilot

Arcade

Skeeball

Air hockey

Miniature golf

Go-kart racing

Game on!

Play hard.

Be a good sport.

Keep your eye on the ball.

Keep your head in the game.

Zooming

Turbo-charged

I'm a heartbeat

Lightning quick

Faster than light

Joystick

Cartridge

Remote control

Online gaming

Video game system

Fishing pole

Motor boat

Fishing line

Can of worms

Bait and tackle

Martial arts

Black belt

Kickboxing

Fitness training

Judo and karate

Dinosaur

Velociraptor

Pterodactyl

Brontosaurus

Tyrannosaurus Rex

Magic show

Card trick

Assistant

Vanishing act

Rabbit from hat

Boys only!

Do not enter!

Private area!

Keep out!

Danger zone!

Boy's clubhouse

Warning – danger!

No trespassing!

No girls allowed.

Boys rule!

Astronomy

Telescope

Galaxy

Black hole

Supernova

Solar System

Mercury and Venus

Earth and Mars

Jupiter and Saturn

Uranus and Neptune

Part 2 Sentences

Part 2 Instructions: First trace each phrase and then copy the sentence onto the blank line below.

Rah! Rah! Rah!

Let's go, team!

Support the home team.

Make the crowd roar.

Strikeout the opponent.

Turn a double play.

Hit a grand slam.

Steal second base.

Knock it out of the park.

Aaarrrggghhh!

Ahoy, mateys!

Yo ho ho, 'tis a pirate's life.

Where's the treasure chest

filled with gold and jewels?

Soccer, anyone?

Don't use your hands.

Kick the ball.

Pass it to a teammate.

Block the goal.

Fly in a spaceship.

Go to the moon.

Travel through outer space.

Visit another world.

The sky is the limit.

Start a bug collection:

ant farm, grasshopper,

tarantula, spiders, beetles,

caterpillar, butterfly,

worms, or a centipede.

Football positions:

quarterback, tackle, safety,

running back, fullback,

tight end, center, linebacker,

wide receiver, and guards.

Go to the zoo today: See

lions, tigers, bears, giraffes,

elephants, a hippopotamus,

zebras, turtles, alligators,

crocodiles, and rams.

Shoot some hoops:

basketball, backboard, net,

guard, forward, center,

offense, defense, pass, block,

lay up, slam dunk.

My mom enrolled me

at the Magic and

Wizardry Elementary

School. I love doing my

homework. It's so cool!

Play hard! Wake up early.

Be active all day long.

Run like the wind.

Spend time with friends.

Don't hold back.

Rainy day activities:

Play board games, watch

television, solve a puzzle,

play video games, or

read a comic book.

Become a magician.

Learn magic tricks.

Guess which card.

Make a coin vanish.

Use magic words.

Build a racetrack.

Include a loop.

Race cars and trucks.

Which one will win?

Make a pit stop.

Robots are so cool.

Maybe I can make one

that will do my chores

for me, while another one

does my homework...

Make an obstacle course.

Run through tires.

Crawl through a tunnel.

Swing across a stream.

Climb over a wall.

Just clowning around!

Such a joker!

Always good for a laugh!

Keeping me entertained!

Just make me chuckle.

I want to meet a wizard.

He could show me magic,

teach me tricks, send me

on a quest, or give me

special powers.

Pets are fun to have.

Kittens and puppies like to

play. Parakeets and parrots

will talk to you. Dogs will

lick your face.

Let's play ball! Kick it,

hit it with a bat, slap it,

spike it, throw it, catch it,

use your head, or shoot it.

Keep your eye on the ball.

Snowboarding sounds

like a fun way to spend

time with friends! Meet

me at the top of the

snow-covered mountain.

Snack time! Candy, chips,

cookies, cupcakes, muffins,

ice-cream, pie, cake, fruit,

donuts, sunflower seeds,

pretzels, or bagels?

Are you afraid of Friday,

the thirteenth? This fear

has two names. Call it

paraskevidekatriaphobia or

friggatriskaidekaphobia.

Gear up to go bike

riding with friends on

Saturday morning.

Next weekend we will

go mountain bike riding.

Visit an ancient castle.

See knights in armor.

Watch them joust.

Tour the castle.

Dungeons are creepy.

Happy birthday!

In the party zone!

Fun times ahead!

Surprises and presents!

Game mode!

It's time to start your

engines. Here they go!

Who has the fastest car?

Look at those cars go!

Zoooooooommmmmmm!

Accelerate all the way!

How fast can you go?

One lap to go!

Checkered flag, here I come!

Heading to Victory Lane!

Nice sports car!

Check out that engine.

Leather interior is sweet.

How many horsepower?

What a sweet ride!

I love my math class.

Arithmetic is easy.

Infinity is a cool concept.

Prime numbers are neat.

Shapes and patterns rule!

Which musical

instruments can you play:

piano, organ, guitar, banjo,

drums, flute, trumpet,

saxophone, or clarinet?

Friday is movie night.

Watch an action scene.

Laugh during a comedy.

Go to space with sci-fi.

See the magic of wizards.

Give it your best shot.

Yes, I can do it!

Be your very best.

Have a positive attitude.

Think happy thoughts.

What's your favorite sport?

Football, basketball, tennis,

baseball, hockey, soccer,

golf, frisbee, volleyball,

or track and field?

Part 3 Just Copy

Part 3 Instructions: Copy these sentences onto the blank lines. (There is no tracing in Part 3.)

Why does junk food taste

so good? You know, the

potato chips, soda, donuts,

candy, and ice-cream?

Ride the biggest, wildest,

fastest roller coaster.

Hang on tight!

It will reach speeds of over

a hundred miles per hour.

How high can you climb?

Mount Everest is the

tallest mountain in

the world. It is 29,029

feet above sea level.

Dinosaurs are cool!

Tyrannosaurus Rex, or

T-Rex is known as the

king of the dinosaurs.

Too bad they are extinct...

Spinosaurus means spine

lizard. It is estimated

they weighed up to twenty

tons, and were up to

fifty-nine feet long.

The stegosaurus dinosaur

was over thirty feet long,

but its brain was the

size of a walnut or

ping pong ball!

No lifeguard on duty!

Swim at your own risk!

A great white shark

was spotted off the coast.

Beach is temporarily closed!

Did you know that a

great white shark has

up to three-hundred

teeth? Don't let one

take a bite out of you!

Send me to the moon!

All systems go. Ten, nine,

eight, seven, six, five, four,

three, two, one. Blast off!

It was a successful launch.

Take me to the baseball

game. Watch my favorite

player. Catch a foul ball.

See a homerun. Eat some

crackerjacks and a hot dog.

Put a quarter in the arcade

game. Master the controls.

Earn an extra man.

Make that quarter last.

Get the high score.

Boys just want to have

fun, fun, fun!

Hang out with friends

on the weekend.

Boys will be boys!

Let's meet at the park.

We can shoot baskets,

play tennis, throw a

baseball, or maybe

just run like crazy!

Watch an extreme and

adventurous sport

like hand gliding,

extreme snowboarding,

or base jumping.

Let's go on a pirate

treasure hunt! Where

will the clues lead to?

Maybe to a treasure chest

filled with chocolate coins.

Classes for the School of

Magical Spells will

begin on October thirty-

first, at twilight.

Bring your cape and wand.

Take your four-by-four

remote control truck to

the off-road races.

Maybe you can take

home the trophy!

Let's have a campout

in my backyard and

sleep in a tent.

We will tell ghost stories

and eat smores.

Sunday is family day.

We like to go hiking or

watch a fun movie.

A bar-b-que get together

is also fun.

I hope my mom doesn't

buy a seedless watermelon

because I want to have

a seed spitting contest.

I think I'll be the winner.

After the sun sets, we

can play flashlight tag.

Tag... You are it!

Do you think we could

catch lightning bugs?

Don't let the spooks in

the haunted house scare

you! It's sure to be

spine-tingling and

very creepy!

Have you hugged your

zombie today? Just

don't let the zombie bite

you! Give him a bloodsicle

to keep him happy!

Meet me at the food

court for pizza, hamburger,

and french fries.

Don't forget the candy

and ice-cream!

Summertime is a good

time to ride the waves,

have a crab race,

build a sand castle, or

bury your feet in the sand.

On a hot summer day,

run through the sprinklers!

Join your friends at

the water park for a

full day of fun!

My sister likes to sun

bathe at the pool so

my friends and I do

cannonballs until we

get her wet!

Walking on stilts so

I will be six feet tall!

Try walking on stilts

through a challenging

obstacle course! It's fun!

Poor little Pluto!

Pluto used to be classified as

a planet, but has been

demoted to a dwarf planet.

Now there are eight planets.

On April Fool's Day,

my mother put green

food coloring in our milk.

That was so gross!

I couldn't eat my cereal.

Stay away from all the

things that go bump in

the night: Ghosts, ghouls,

walking corpses, creepy

critters, and vampire bats.

Whistle for my dog to

come so we can play

fetch, tug of war, frisbee

toss, or chase. Dogs are

great companions.

What is your favorite

ice-cream flavor? Is

it vanilla, chocolate chip,

rocky road, Neapolitan,

or cookies and cream?

Archery is fun once you

get the hang of it. At

first it is hard to even

hit the target. I love

hitting the bull's-eye!

Watch the pros kayak

through the white water

rapids. It is sure to give

you white knuckles!

It's an adrenaline rush!

Would you dive in with

sharks? How about

scuba diving to explore an

old shipwreck? That sounds

like fun! Take pictures!

Let's go climb a tree!

Not just any tree, but the

tallest one in the

neighborhood. Who can

get to the top first?

My friends and I make

paper gliders.

We have a contest to

see which one flies the

highest, and the farthest.

Squirt guns are a blast!

I want the biggest and

the best so when we have

water fights I will totally

soak my friends!

Why do we need so much

sleep? There are so many

things I could be doing!

Don't tell my mom, but

I make excuses to stay up!

When I have a sleep over,

we tell ghost stories.

We try to scare each other

so bad that no one can

get to sleep!

It's a zombie apocalypse!

Should we try to run and

hide, or fight them?

What would you do?

We should have a plan!

Doing well at school.

Getting good grades.

Parents are proud.

Way to go! You go boy!

Feeling fantastic!

Soccer is one of the most

popular team sports.

You don't have time to get

bored. You will probably

run a few miles.

Zipping along on my

inline skates!

Skating to our neighborhood

skating park to celebrate

my best friend's birthday.

Be creative!

Let your imagination go!

Join a music, drama,

art, or dance club.

Enjoy your artistic abilities!

It is family night at the

bowling alley.

I hope to throw all

spares and strikes!

Don't throw a gutter ball!

Are you hungry for

macaroni and cheese, pizza,

hot dogs, spaghetti and

meatballs, tacos, or a

peanut butter sandwich?

Now it's time for dessert!

What should I have?

Chocolate chip cookies, cake,

an ice-cream cone, or a

hot fudge sundae?

I can't wait to go to the

amusement park so I can

ride the Ferris wheel,

bumper cars, roller coaster,

teacups, and the swings.

Let's play twenty questions.

Charades is a fun family

game to play.

Button, button... Who

has the button?

Summertime camping

adventures include a

campfire, roasted

marshmallows, and

sleeping under the stars.

Wow! You did it!

Awesome! Super-duper!

Cursive writing is fun!

Sign your name below.

Your name is _____

Other Workbooks by Julie Harper

✓ *Letters, Words, and Silly Phrases Handwriting Workbook (Reproducible): Practice Writing in Cursive (Second and Third Grade).*

✓ *Wacky Sentences Handwriting Workbook (Reproducible): Practice Writing in Cursive (Third and Fourth Grade).*

✓ Print Uppercase and Lowercase Letters, Words, and Silly Phrases: Kindergarten and First Grade Writing Practice Workbook (Reproducible).

✓ Print Wacky Sentences: First and Second Grade Writing Practice Workbook (Reproducible).

✓ *Cursive Handwriting Workbook for Girls.*

✓ *Cursive Handwriting Practice Workbook for Teens.*

✓ *Spooky Cursive Handwriting Practice Workbook.*

✓ *Cursive Handwriting Practice Workbook for Boys.*

✓ Princess Printing Practice Writing Workbook for Girls.

✓ Sports Printing Practice Writing Workbook for Boys.

✓ Tongue Twisters Printing Practice Writing Workbook.

✓ Read Wacky Sentences Basic Reading Comprehension Workbook.

✓ Wacky Creative Writing Assignments Workbook.

Made in the USA
San Bernardino, CA
19 May 2016